PLAYA DEL CARMEN TRAVEL GUIDE 2024

The Complete Handbook to Exploring Playa del Carmen's Beautiful Sights, History, Food, and Culture.

JACK MILIGAN

TABLE OF CONTENTS

INTRODUCTION

Welcome to Playa del Carmen, a captivating gem on Mexico's Caribbean coast, where pristine white sands are embraced by turquoise waters, and quaint streets pulse with the lively pulse of the local culture. With the help of this travel guide, we hope you will discover the charms of Playa del Carmen, a place that skillfully combines the calm of immaculate beaches with the energy of a bustling town.

As you set out on this adventure, explore the ruins of ancient civilizations at the nearby Mayan ruins, or just relax on Playa del Carmen Beach's sun-kissed shores. Walk along Fifth Avenue, where a rainbow of stores, restaurants, and hidden gems await discovery. Take part in thrilling water sports in the Caribbean Sea's azure depths or indulge in mouthwateringly authentic Mexican cuisine.

Playa del Carmen is known for its stunning scenery and perfect beaches, but it's also known for its rich cultural tapestry that combines modern and Mayan traditions. Every corner of the place has a story waiting to be discovered, from the upbeat beat of the local music to the striking colors of the indigenous crafts.

Irrespective of your preferences for a carefree getaway, an action-packed vacation, or a cultural immersion, Playa del Carmen welcomes you to immerse yourself in a mosaic of unforgettable experiences. This guide will help you discover the hidden gems of this idyllic coastal location, making your trip more than just a trip; it will help you create a lifetime of treasured memories. Greetings from Playa del Carmen, a place where the Caribbean whispers legends of splendor and adventure.

Playa del Carmen's History

Playa del Carmen, which is tucked away on the Yucatán Peninsula's sun-drenched shores, has a fascinating history that is as captivating as its turquoise waters. Ancient civilizations rose and fell near this coastal gem long before it became a sought-after destination for adventurers and sun-seekers.

Roots in Maya
The history of Playa del Carmen starts with the Mayans, who lived in the area as early as 2000 BCE. There is still evidence of them in the nearby archaeological sites of Coba and Tulum. These prehistoric people established coastal settlements that flourished for centuries because

they were drawn to the region's fertile lands and abundant marine life.

Hub for Trade

The Mayans relied heavily on Playa del Carmen as a trading post during the Postclassic era (1000–1500 CE). Its advantageous position along the coast's trade routes made it easier to exchange products like cocoa, jade, and obsidian. The lively atmosphere of the town is still resonant with the sounds of this thriving trade.

Historical Heritage

Early in the 16th century, Playa del Carmen changed with the entrance of Spanish conquistadors. The once-thriving Mayan settlements began to decline as a result of diseases brought by European settlers. The town itself remained a sleepy fishing community, overshadowed by the nearby port of Cozumel.

Village for Fishing to Tourist Haven

Playa del Carmen continued to exist modestly for centuries, mostly as a fishing destination. The town didn't transform into the thriving tourist destination it is today until the latter half of the 20th century. A turning point was reached in the 1970s with the completion of the ferry dock that connected Playa del Carmen to Cozumel.

Boom in Tourism

Adventurers were drawn to the spotless beaches and proximity to historic ruins as the ferry revolutionized accessibility. In short order, Playa del Carmen became a refuge for travelers looking for a real Mexican experience. The town's fame grew over the next few decades, and it managed to maintain its cultural authenticity while developing into a popular tourist destination.

A Marvel of Today

Playa del Carmen is a living example of how history and modernity can coexist peacefully today. This is where Quintana Roo's cultural heartbeats, as seen by the lively street art, authentic marketplaces, and continued practice of Mayan customs. The town's expansion has enriched rather than erased its history, weaving a dynamic tapestry that is revealed with every step on its cobblestone streets.

Every grain of sand in Playa del Carmen holds a piece of its rich history, so keep that in mind as you explore the sun-kissed beaches and venture into the bustling streets. The past is not a far-off memory but rather a vital component of the present in this idyllic coastal town. Welcome to Playa del Carmen, a place where the passing of time has molded a place's resilience, trade, and enduring spirit into whispers in the sand.

CHAPTER ONE: PREPARATION

The Ideal Season to Visit Playa del Carmen

Traveling to Playa del Carmen requires not only a wanderlust but also a calculated decision about when to visit to fully appreciate the coastal charm. This tropical paradise is tucked away on Mexico's Caribbean coast and boasts a year-round climate that offers different settings for all kinds of travelers.

December to April (High Season Bliss):
The high season, which runs from December to April, is a dream come true for those looking for the ultimate sun-drenched getaway. Blue skies, mild breezes, and temperatures between the mid-70s and low 90s Fahrenheit (24–34°C) greet guests at Playa del Carmen. The Caribbean's azure waters are perfect for snorkeling, diving, and leisurely dips during the dry season.

Many travelers from North America and Europe take their winter vacation during this time, so expect a lively atmosphere. The town is lively and the beaches come alive with a rainbow of sun worshippers, providing a colorful backdrop for travelers who enjoy the social aspect of travel.

May to June, September to November (Shoulder Seasons):
The shoulder seasons reveal a different side to Playa del Carmen. The dry season ends in May or June and is followed by the rainy season, which brings sporadic downpours that change the verdant surroundings. The official hurricane season runs from September to November, although there is still a chance of storms. But these times also mean fewer people, calmer streets, and more reasonably priced lodging options.

The shoulder seasons might be especially interesting to tourists who enjoy off-the-beaten-path experiences. Nature lovers can see how the landscape changes and the chance to explore Playa del Carmen in a more private setting frequently outweighs the risk of rain.

July to August (Summer Glow):
In Playa del Carmen, summer casts a warm, radiant glow over the area. Even though it can get very hot—between the mid-70s and upper 90s Fahrenheit (24–35°C)—the cool Caribbean Sea is calling for relief. Water sports enthusiasts and those looking for a balance between vibrant energy and less crowds will find that this season is perfect.

The town comes alive with a festive spirit as the sun descends. Beachside celebrations, street performers, and local musicians all add to the vibrant atmosphere that characterizes a summer vacation in Playa del Carmen.

Your preferences and travel objectives will ultimately determine the ideal time to visit Playa del Carmen. Playa del Carmen welcomes you year-round, whether you're looking for the bright pulse of high season, the serene serenity of shoulder seasons, or the radiant glow of summer. So prepare your belongings, set your compass, and allow the rhythm of the Caribbean to lead you to the ideal location in this idyllic seaside resort.

Traveling to Playa del Carmen

Taking a strategic approach to transportation is necessary when starting the adventure that awaits in Playa del Carmen. This beach paradise, which is located on Mexico's breathtaking Caribbean coast, provides several ways for visitors to get to its sandy shores, making the trip there as easy as the destination is magical.

Flying to Paradise:
Flying is the most popular and effective way for visitors from abroad to get to Playa del Carmen. Cancún

International Airport (CUN), which is about 34 miles (55 km) north of Playa del Carmen, is the closest. This convenient gateway is served by well-connected airports that welcome flights from major cities across the globe.

Once in Cancún, visitors can take several different modes of transportation to get to Playa del Carmen. Taxis, rental cars, and private airport shuttles are easily accessible and provide comfort and flexibility for the roughly 45-minute ride.

Departing from Nearby Locations by Road:
A fascinating option if you're already in Mexico or the Yucatán Peninsula is road travel. Highways connect Playa del Carmen, and taking a road trip gives you a chance to see the varied scenery of this fascinating area.

Rental cars give you freedom and the opportunity to go wherever you want, at your speed, whether you're traveling from Cancún, Tulum, or other nearby locations. As an alternative, the comfortable and dependable ADO buses provide a reasonably priced and picturesque ride.

A Journey Around the Seas from Cozumel:
If you'd prefer a more nautical approach, you can get to Playa del Carmen by boat from the neighboring island of Cozumel. Ferries provide a scenic ride across the

Caribbean's turquoise waters regularly between Cozumel and Playa del Carmen.

In addition to offering a picturesque introduction to the coastal beauty, the ferry ride facilitates a smooth transition between two of the most popular locations in the Yucatán. Playa del Carmen's lively atmosphere beckons as you disembark, promising an instant immersion in its charm.

Getting Around on Local Transit:
Navigating Playa del Carmen and its environs is effortless once you're there. Its small size makes it easy to explore on foot, and you can add even more flexibility by renting scooters or bicycles. Local buses and taxis are also widely accessible for individuals seeking a prompt and effective means of transportation.

Traveling to Playa del Carmen is the beginning of an experience that is yet to come. Choosing between the ease of flying, the liberty of driving, or the seaside allure of taking a ferry ride can lead to a variety of experiences and sights. So, prepare for your wanderlust, pick your favorite means of transportation, and let the trip to Playa del Carmen be just as exciting as the final destination.

Visa and Entry Requirements

Traveling to Playa del Carmen's sun-kissed shores requires more than just sunscreen and an adventurous spirit. A seamless transition from your home country to this coastal haven on Mexico's Caribbean coast is ensured by understanding the requirements for visas and entry.

Easy Entry:
Traveling to Mexico is a simple process for nationals of many different countries. Visa-free entry is permitted by the Mexican government for brief visits, usually up to 180 days. This kind of policy makes it easier for tourists to visit Playa del Carmen and enjoy its beaches, cultural attractions, and lively atmosphere.

Essential Passport:
Although many people may not need a visa, having a current passport is a must. Make sure that your passport is valid for at least six months after the date you intend to leave Mexico. You can concentrate on the adventures that lie ahead in Playa del Carmen with this precaution, which guarantees a seamless entry and exit process.

Visitor ID for Extended Stays:
If you intend to stay longer than the first 180 days on vacation, you must get a Tourist Card. This card can be

obtained at the airport or border crossing under the name Forma Migratoria Multiple (FMM). It's a simple procedure that entails completing a form and paying a charge to extend your visa-free period beyond the first one.

Needs for Certain Nationalities to Obtain a Visa:
Even though many travelers can enter without a visa, it's important to confirm the requirements specific to your country of citizenship. Even for brief visits, some nations may need a visa, so it's important to check this well in advance. The most recent information on visa requirements and application procedures can be obtained from the Mexican embassy or consulate in your country of residence.

Visas for Work and Business:
A valid visa is essential for anyone planning business-related travel or prolonged stays for work. Mexico provides several different types of visas, each with its own requirements and application procedures, such as work and business visas. Consult the Mexican embassy or consulate and start the application process well in advance of the dates you intend to travel.

Medical and Travel Insurance:
Getting comprehensive health and travel insurance is a wise move for any traveler, even if a visa is not required.

Like any destination, Playa del Carmen has its share of unanticipated events. Having insurance makes sure you're covered in case of accidents, trip delays, or other unanticipated circumstances.

It takes careful planning, knowledge of the requirements, and appropriate documentation to ensure a seamless entry into Playa del Carmen. Having your documentation in order lets you concentrate on the magic of your trip, rather than worrying about paperwork when you're lounging on the beaches or touring Mayan ruins. Thus, make sure your passport is up to date, familiarize yourself with the necessary documents for a visa, and get ready for an incredible journey in Playa del Carmen, a coastal paradise.

Handling Money in Playa del Carmen

Understanding the local currency and adopting wise budgeting strategies will not only improve your trip experience but also let you enjoy the beach paradise without worrying about money when you visit the lively Playa del Carmen. Come with me as we explore the realm of pesos, haggling, and inexpensive treats.

The Peso:

Before entering the bustling streets of Playa del Carmen, it's a good idea to become familiar with the denominations of the Mexican Peso (MXN), which is the country's official currency. Even though some places do take major credit cards, you'll be able to easily navigate local markets, street vendors, and small businesses if you have a pocket full of pesos.

Using Cash or Card:
It's a good idea to have some cash on hand, even though credit cards are generally accepted in larger establishments—especially for smaller transactions and in more intimate settings. You can easily get pesos out of an ATM in Playa del Carmen whenever you need to. Remember that some businesses might give you a discount if you pay with cash, so it can be helpful to have a variety of payment options.

Basics of Bargaining:
Don't be scared to master the art of haggling as you peruse the markets and interact with neighborhood vendors. In Playa del Carmen, especially in markets like Fifth Avenue, haggling is a common practice. Channel your inner negotiator and take advantage of the cultural exchange that comes with it. Courtesy and a friendly manner go a long way in securing good deals.

A Taste of Heaven on a Budget:

All price ranges can enjoy the culinary adventure that Playa del Carmen has to offer. In addition to the town's many fine dining establishments, there are a ton of local restaurants and street food vendors where you can sample real food without going over budget. Explore beyond the popular tourist destinations to find undiscovered treasures offering delicious tamales, tacos, and other Mexican delicacies.

Affordability of Accommodations:
Playa del Carmen offers lodging options ranging from luxurious resorts to affordable hostels, catering to a wide variety of tourists. Choosing accommodations outside of the main tourist areas can reveal quaint boutique hotels and quaint guesthouses that offer comfort and value for money.

Transportation:
Traveling around Playa del Carmen doesn't have to break the bank. Exploring the town on foot is a pleasure, and renting a bike or scooter provides an economical and effective way to get around. An additional affordable way to get to neighboring towns and attractions is by public bus.

Tipping Protocol:
In Playa del Carmen, tipping is expected. If service is not included, it is customary to leave a 10-15% gratuity in

restaurants. A little gratuity is greatly appreciated and goes a long way toward showing gratitude for other services, like taxi rides and tour guides.

You will not only stretch your pesos further by learning the local language, mastering the art of haggling, and implementing astute budgeting strategies, but you will also become more fully immersed in the culture. Playa del Carmen welcomes you to enjoy every second of your stay, from bargain dining to discovering one-of-a-kind finds in neighborhood markets. So, bring your adventurous spirit and financial acumen, and watch as Playa del Carmen, a coastal paradise, presents itself to you as an affordable opera of experiences.

CHAPTER TWO: ACCOMMODATION

Top Playa del Carmen Hotels and Resorts

The variety of lodging options in Playa del Carmen matches the wide range of experiences this idyllic coastal town has to offer as soon as you enter its enchanted realm. Playa del Carmen offers lodging options to suit every preference, from lavish resorts tucked away along immaculate beaches to boutique hotels tucked into the bustling center of the town. This is a carefully selected list of some of the best hotels and resorts that guarantee a lavish embrace of the coastal charm in addition to a great place to stay.

Rosewood Mayakoba
Rosewood Mayakoba is a luxurious haven that perfectly melds with the surrounding area's natural beauty, nestled within the lush embrace of the Mayakoba jungle. This resort is a haven for those looking for an intimate and exclusive experience thanks to its private plunge pools, overwater lagoon suites, and unmatched service.

Mayakoba Banyan Tree:

Nestled amidst the meandering canals of Mayakoba, Banyan Tree provides a tranquil haven with its breathtaking overwater villas and verdant surroundings. The resort offers a superb fusion of luxury and environmental awareness thanks to its eco-friendly design, which reflects its dedication to sustainability.

Grand Hyatt Playa del Carmen Resort:
Grand Hyatt Playa del Carmen Resort, a beachfront haven that blends modern architecture with Mexican flair, is perched on the immaculate Playa Mamitas. This resort is a seamless blend of excitement and relaxation, with its infinity pools, the vibrant energy of Fifth Avenue, and breathtaking ocean views.

Mahekal Beach Resort:
Mahekal Beach Resort's thatched-roof palapas, colorful décor, and ideal beachfront location epitomize bohemian charm. The resort's easy access to Playa del Carmen's vibrant cultural scene is combined with a laid-back vibe.

Thompson Playa del Carmen:
The height of stylish sophistication, Thompson Playa del Carmen is the perfect getaway for city dwellers. This boutique hotel, which is situated on the famous Fifth Avenue, has a lively nightlife scene close by, rooftop pools with panoramic views, and sleek design.

Viceroy Riviera Maya:

Viceroy Riviera Maya, tucked away in Playa del Carmen's verdant jungles, radiates personal elegance. This resort invites guests to relax in the embrace of nature with its private villas, outdoor showers, and personalized service, all contributing to its atmosphere of seclusion and luxury.

Fairmont Mayakoba:

Fairmont Mayakoba is the ideal combination of opulence and family-friendly features. It features vast grounds, interconnected waterways, and a special kids' program. This resort ensures a harmonious balance between leisure and recreation, making it the perfect getaway for families.

Playa del Carmen's lodging options satisfy the varied needs of every visitor, whether they are looking for the urban sophistication of boutique hotels, the secluded luxury of overwater villas, or the bohemian charm of beachfront resorts. Every hotel and resort offers guests a comfortable stay as well as a gateway to this coastal haven's distinct charm. Thus, pick your haven carefully and allow Playa del Carmen's magic to unfold inside the sumptuous confines of your lodging of choice.

Budget-Friendly Playa del Carmen Lodging Options

There are many affordable hotel options in Playa del Carmen for the discerning traveler who wants to enjoy the sun-kissed beaches without going over budget. These lodging options, which range from quaint guesthouses to comfortable hostels, offer not only an affordable stay but also an authentic window into the local way of life. This is a carefully selected list of affordable places to stay that guarantee a comfortable stay without sacrificing the charm of this idyllic coastal town.

Hostel 3B:
Hostel 3B, conveniently located in the center of Playa del Carmen, offers a lively atmosphere at an affordable price. With its shared areas and dormitory-style rooms, this hostel is ideal for people traveling alone or looking for a social experience. Easy access to Fifth Avenue and the town's exciting nightlife is ensured by its central location.

Selina Playa del Carmen:
Travelers on a tight budget can find a bohemian-chic getaway in Selina Playa del Carmen. This hostel has a relaxed atmosphere and offers both private rooms and dorms as forms of lodging. A communal kitchen and

common spaces with artwork from the area's artists enhance the feeling of belonging.

Hacienda Maria Bonita:
Budget-friendly rooms in a lovely setting are available at Hacienda Maria Bonita for those seeking a hint of authentic Mexican culture. Just off Fifth Avenue, this guesthouse perfectly captures the cultural essence of Playa del Carmen without breaking the bank.

Maya del Carmen Hotel:
The Hotel Maya del Carmen provides comfort without sacrificing simplicity. Conveniently located near Fifth Avenue and the beach, this affordable hotel offers an ideal starting point for exploring. It's the perfect option for budget-conscious travelers looking for neat, comfortable rooms.

La Tortuga Hotel & Spa:
In the middle of the busy town, the La Tortuga Hotel & Spa provides a tranquil haven. This affordable choice offers a calm haven close to Playa del Carmen's lively energy, complete with a courtyard pool and cozy accommodations.

Hotel Plaza Phocea:
Conveniently located in the center of Playa del Carmen, Hotel Plaza Phocea is an affordable choice without

sacrificing comfort. This hotel offers easy access to the town's beaches and attractions and simple but comfortable rooms.

Fashion Hotel & Spa:
The inexpensive stay with a contemporary flair is provided by In Fashion Hotel & Spa for those looking for affordability without sacrificing a hint of elegance. It stands out as a great option for travelers on a tight budget who appreciate style thanks to its convenient location, spa, and elegant accommodations.

The affordable lodging options available in Playa del Carmen provide access to a variety of experiences without breaking the bank. These lodging options show that you don't have to sacrifice comfort or the allure of this coastal paradise for a budget trip, regardless of your preference for the lively social atmosphere of a hostel, the bohemian-chic vibe of a guesthouse, or the straightforwardness of a low-cost hotel. So, bring your spirit of thrift and your sense of adventure, and let Playa del Carmen reveal itself within the shelter of affordable havens.

Unique Places to Stay in Playa del Carmen

Entering the enthralling realm of Playa del Carmen, the town provides a multitude of unique lodging options in addition to its vibrant streets and sun-kissed beaches. Playa del Carmen offers a variety of accommodations that guarantee an experience beyond the ordinary, from eco-friendly retreats nestled in the natural surroundings to boutique hotels with a touch of local charm. This is a carefully selected selection of lodgings that provide more than just a spot to sleep; they offer an immersive experience that becomes an essential part of your trip.

La Selva Mariposa:
At La Selva Mariposa, get away from it all and take in the beauty of the jungle. This eco-friendly glamping location offers opulent tents surrounded by lush vegetation. Your lullaby is the sound of rustling leaves and the calls of exotic birds, providing a special fusion of comfort and the natural world.

Encanto Riviera:
Encanto Riviera provides a boutique experience that blends elegance and artistic flair for those looking for a vacation that is a work of art in and of itself. Every room reflects the artistic vibe of Playa del Carmen with its vivid colors and modern design. Easy access to the

town's cultural attractions is ensured by its central location.

Ko'ox Downtown Family Boutique Hotel:
Experience the warm and welcoming culture of Mexico at Ko'ox Downtown Family Boutique Hotel. Guests are welcomed with warmth and a feeling of familial care in this cozy lodging. Cozy accommodations with traditional Mexican decor combined with attentive service make it feel like you're visiting family.

Habitas Tulum:
Though not located in Playa del Carmen itself, Habitas Tulum is an eco-friendly haven that can be found just a short drive away from Tulum. Nestled against the Caribbean Sea, this eco-friendly hideaway combines beachside luxury with a strong commitment to environmental awareness. This is a unique coastal haven with private beachfront casitas and communal spaces meant for connection.

The Palm at Playa:
One distinctive feature of The Palm at Playa is its rooftop oasis, which offers expansive views of the Caribbean Sea. This small hotel offers contemporary elegance combined with a dash of regional character. The rooftop lounge and pool offer a distinctive view of

Playa del Carmen and transform into a haven above the busy town.

Nomade Tulum:
A short drive south to Tulum will take you to Nomade, a wellness retreat with a bohemian vibe that offers accommodations beyond the norm. Nomade Tulum offers an immersive experience centered around well-being and connection with nature through its yoga classes, holistic spa treatments, and thoughtfully designed beachfront accommodations.

The distinctive lodging options in Playa del Carmen transform your visit from a place to stay into a memorable part of your journey. Whether you go for boutique elegance, wellness retreat, or jungle glamping, these accommodations provide more than just a place to sleep; they become a blank canvas for the tales you will take back with you. Thus, let your lodging embody your spirit of exploration, and allow Playa del Carmen to emerge via the prism of these unique visits, each contributing a new dimension to the overall picture of your seaside sojourn.

CHAPTER THREE: EXPLORATION

Playa del Carmen's Beaches and Water Sports

Water lovers and sun worshippers alike are drawn to Playa del Carmen by its immaculate stretches of sandy shores that are caressed by the Caribbean Sea's turquoise waters. Playa del Carmen's beaches and water sports provide a wide range of experiences that capture the spirit of this coastal paradise, whether you're itching for the excitement of underwater exploration or just a peaceful day by the water.

Playa del Carmen Beach:
Without a doubt, Playa del Carmen's name beach is its greatest asset. Playa del Carmen Beach, which stretches along the town's shoreline, offers a picture-perfect scene with its powdery sand and crystal-clear waters. When you take a stroll along the shore or soak up the sun's rays, feel the soft embrace of the sand beneath your feet.

Extreme Water Sports:
Playa del Carmen is a water sports playground for the daring. The second-largest coral reef system in the

world, the Mesoamerican Barrier Reef, offers snorkelers and divers a vibrant underwater world to explore. Great diving locations can be found on the neighboring island of Cozumel, which is easily reached by ferry.

Cenote Adventure:
Beyond the salted embrace of the Caribbean, Playa del Carmen is encircled by an enigmatic system of cenotes, which are naturally occurring sinkholes that contain freshwater that is crystal clear. Enjoy a cool dip in one of these cenotes, like Cenote Dos Ojos or Cenote Azul, and be amazed by the underground splendor that nature's creative artistry has produced.

Jet Skiing and Parasailing:
Playa del Carmen's beaches provide jet skiing and parasailing experiences for those in need of an adrenaline rush. Enjoy the wind in your hair as you soar above the coastline on a parasailing excursion that offers breathtaking views of the town and its environs, or feel the rush of the waves as you jet ski across them.

Fishing Excursions:
Cast your line into the Caribbean's bountiful waters to start a fishing expedition. Playa del Carmen offers deep-sea fishing trips that could reward you with a plentiful catch, ranging from marlin to snapper, regardless of your level of experience.

Catamaran and Yacht Cruises: Glimmering in Sunset Bliss:

Sail along the coast in style and comfort on a yacht or catamaran cruise. These cruises offer the perfect environment for taking in the splendor of the Caribbean Sea while indulging in delicious food and revitalizing drinks. Activities range from romantic sunset sails to snorkeling excursions during the day.

The beaches and water sports in Playa del Carmen combine to create a peaceful and exciting symphony of adventure and relaxation. Whether you're enjoying exhilarating water sports, exploring underwater treasures, or simply relaxing on the silky sands, Playa del Carmen's coastal charm unfurls in the rhythmic embrace of the Caribbean Sea. So take a plunge into the blue ocean, let the surf soothe your senses, and let Playa del Carmen's coastal magic envelope you in an evocative underwater symphony.

Exploring the Rich Culture of Playa del Carmen

Beyond the brightly colored sands and crystal-clear waters, Playa del Carmen reveals a rich tapestry of cultural attractions that invite visitors to delve into the town's colorful past. Playa del Carmen welcomes you to go on a cultural odyssey that blends the past with the present, creating an immersive experience that leaves a lasting impression on those who venture into its cultural embrace. This journey takes you from ancient Mayan ruins to vibrant local markets.

Mayan Ruins:
The ruins of the ancient Mayan civilization are located not far from Playa del Carmen. Tulum provides an enthralling trip through time, perched majestically atop cliffs overlooking the Caribbean Sea. Discover the remarkably preserved buildings and temples that serve as reminders of the Mayans' architectural mastery and cultural importance.

Chichen Itzá:
The famous Chichen Itzá is a must-see cultural wonder, even though it's a little further from Playa del Carmen. The magnificence of Mayan civilization is on display at this UNESCO World Heritage Site, which is also one of the New Seven Wonders of the World. El Castillo, popularly known as the Kukulkan Pyramid, is a monument to sophisticated architectural style and cutting-edge astronomical knowledge.

Local Marketplaces:

Playa del Carmen's main thoroughfare, La Quinta Avenida, also known as Fifth Avenue, is crowded with lively stores and restaurants. Visit the neighborhood markets where craftspeople display their work and sell handmade textiles, original artwork, and traditional Mexican souvenirs. Explore the vibrant array of hues, sounds, and tastes that characterize the town's cultural core.

Xcaret Park:
The eco-archaeological park Xcaret, which is close to Playa del Carmen, skillfully combines cultural experiences with the natural world. Experience reconstructed Mayan villages, take in customary rituals, and explore underground rivers encircled by stalagmites and stalactites. An immersive journey into the natural and cultural heritage of the area can be had at Xcaret.

Day of the Dead Events:
Should your trip fall between late October and early November, you may be able to take part in Mexico's colorful Day of the Dead festivities. Playa del Carmen comes alive with processions honoring the deceased, vibrant altars, and traditional music. Participate in the celebrations to see how closely Mexicans cling to their heritage.

Cultural Events:

Experience the rich cultural legacy of Playa del Carmen by attending live music and traditional dance performances. You can witness the colorful costumes and upbeat beats that reaffirm centuries of tradition at cultural events held at several locations throughout the city, such as Sabor a Playa and Riviera Art. These events highlight the diversity of Mexican folklore.

Beyond its sun-kissed exterior, Playa del Carmen's cultural attractions weave a captivating tale. Experiences such as touring historic sites, bargaining in neighborhood markets, or taking part in traditional festivals provide a window into the character of this seaside retreat. Allow the rich cultural legacy of Playa del Carmen to lead you as you weave a tale that spans time and immerses you in the essence of Mexico's dynamic past and present.

Playa del Carmen's Dynamic Nightlife

Playa del Carmen changes from a sleepy beach into a vibrant center of entertainment and nightlife when the sun sets. The town's after-dark scene invites night owls and party animals to participate in a varied array of nocturnal adventures, from intimate jazz bars to bustling beachfront clubs, guaranteeing that the spirit of Playa del Carmen endures well into the early hours of the morning.

The Quinta Avenida:

Fifth Avenue, also known as La Quinta Avenida, becomes the center of Playa del Carmen's nightlife. This busy pedestrian street comes alive with the sound of live music, street performers, and partygoers chatting as the moon rises. Wander along the avenue, take in the wide variety of eateries, shops, and bars, and experience the lively vibe that characterizes the town's nighttime pulse.

Beachfront Clubs:

Playa del Carmen features a wide selection of beachside clubs that capitalize on the breathtaking coastal scenery of the town. With their blend of electronic beats and beachside atmosphere, Mamitas Beach Club and Canibal Royal invite guests to dance under the stars while feeling the sand beneath their feet. These locations expertly combine music, refreshing sea breezes, and an energetic crowd to create an amazing beach party atmosphere.

Coco Bongo:

Coco Bongo is a legendary place to have fun if you're looking for a unique night out. This multi-level club combines music, acrobatics, and colorful performances to create a theatrical experience. It's a spectacle that goes beyond what you would find in a typical nightclub, so anyone looking for a show and some fun should check it out.

Sundeck Bars:

Upgrade your evening experience by sipping cocktails and taking in expansive town views from one of Playa del Carmen's rooftop bars. Locations such as The Palm at Playa and the rooftop of the Thompson Hotel are elegant and offer the ideal environment for relaxing and enjoying the town's nightlife.

Live Music Locations:

Take in the heartfelt sounds of live music at the small venues in Playa del Carmen. Latin rhythms and jazz and blues are among the performances held at places like the Riviera Art Gallery and the Karma Bagus Bar. Take in the town's cultural vibrancy while enjoying your favorite beverage and letting the melodies take you elsewhere.

Street Food and Late-Night Dining:

Satisfy your appetite at Playa del Carmen's late-night restaurants and street food vendors as the night draws in. The town's culinary scene is open late, so you can enjoy Mexican cuisine to fuel your nighttime adventures. From flavorful tacos to delicious churros.

The vibrant nightlife and entertainment of Playa del Carmen capture the essence of the town's multiculturalism and liveliness. Every night in Playa del Carmen invites you to celebrate life under the stars, whether you're dancing on the beach, taking in a breathtaking show, or relaxing at a rooftop bar. Allow the nighttime beat to lead you along the streets and coastline, and lose yourself in the enchantment of Playa del Carmen's vibrant after-dark.

CHAPTER FOUR: CUISINE

Discovering Playa del Carmen's Local Mexican Cuisine

In addition to captivating visitors with its immaculate beaches, Playa del Carmen, a Caribbean coastal gem, tantalizes the senses with a gastronomic scene that reflects the depth and variety of Mexican cuisine. The town's restaurants, which range from street tacos to fine dining venues, provide a culinary adventure that enables visitors to experience the true flavor of Mexican food.

Tacos on the Street:
Take a culinary journey through Playa del Carmen's busy streets, where the aroma of freshly made tortillas and sizzling meats fills the air. Tacos from the street are the ultimate treat. These portable marvels, which can be filled with flavorful carnitas, succulent al pastor, or grilled carne asada, highlight the culinary artistry of simplicity in Mexican cuisine.

Ceviche:
Because of its coastal setting, ceviche has become a star in the culinary world in Playa del Carmen. Fresh seafood, usually marinated in lime juice with tomatoes,

onions, and cilantro, makes for a light meal that reflects the charm of the town's waterfront. Ceviche is a must-try for anyone yearning for a burst of coastal freshness, whether it be shrimp or fish.

Mole Poblano:
Explore the rich and flavorful world of mole poblano, a traditional Mexican sauce renowned for its sophisticated fusion of chocolate, spices, and chili peppers. Restaurants in Playa del Carmen serve variations of this culinary masterwork, letting you enjoy the harmonious fusion of spicy, savory, and sweet flavors on your tongue.

Tamales:
A taste of Mexican comfort food can be found in tamales, which are steamed parcels of masa filled with different ingredients. These portable treats, which are typically wrapped in corn husks and packed with sweet or savory meats or chilies, are a testament to a culinary legacy that has been passed down through the years.

A Stuffed Pepper Fiesta with Chiles Rellenos:
A colorful fusion of Mexican flavors, chiles rellenos are made with large poblano peppers filled with a variety of fillings. The peppers are then battered and fried to golden perfection, accompanied by cheeses, meats, nuts, and fruits. When paired with flavorful sauces, Chiles

Rellenos offers a delightful combination of flavors and textures.

Aguas Frescas:
Enjoy Aguas Frescas, cool fruit-infused drinks that are the ideal diversion from the warm coastal weather, to go with the strong flavors of Mexican food. These drinks highlight the varied abundance of Mexican fruits, whether it's the zest of lime, the sweetness of tamarind, or the floral notes of hibiscus (Jamaica).

Churros and Chocolate:
Finish off your dinner adventure with some chocolate and churros. Dipped in rich, velvety chocolate, these deep-fried dough delights, dusted with sugar and cinnamon, become the ideal vehicle. It is a charming conclusion that perfectly captures the tenderness and warmth of Mexican hospitality.

Travelers are invited to a gastronomic fiesta that reflects the town's cultural diversity and lively coastline thanks to the authentic Mexican food of Playa del Carmen. Every morsel is a celebration of Mexico's culinary legacy, whether you're relishing the complexity of mole poblano or the simplicity of street tacos. Go out to the restaurants in the area, sample the flavors that adorn the town's culinary canvas, and allow Playa del Carmen's culinary symphony to become a treasured portion of your travel memoirs.

Discovering Distinct Flavors in Playa del Carmen's International Cuisine

Located on the Caribbean coast, Playa del Carmen is a melting pot of different cultures as well as a haven for Mexican food. There's a wide variety of restaurants along Fifth Avenue and its surrounding streets that serve food from all over the world. Playa del Carmen offers an international dining scene that promises a cross-border culinary adventure, with options ranging from Caribbean-inspired sushi bars to classic Italian trattorias.

Delicious Italian Food; Pizza, Pasta, and More:
Taste your way through Italy without ever leaving Playa del Carmen by indulging in the delicious cuisine of Italian eateries. These restaurants offer the essence of Italian cooking to the Caribbean, from expertly wood-fired pizzas to handcrafted pasta dishes dripping with flavorful sauces.

Caribbean-Style Sushi:
Playa del Carmen's sushi bars provide a delightful experience for those seeking a culinary fusion that combines the vibrant flavors of the Caribbean with the

accuracy of Japanese sushi. Anticipate inventive rolls with tropical fruits, fresh seafood, and distinctive sauces that offer a delectable fusion of flavors from around the world.

French Culinary Complexity:
The French restaurants in Playa del Carmen will add a touch of French elegance to your dining experience. Savor delectable dishes that exhibit culinary artistry, such as delicate pastries and classic coq au vin. You are taken to a Parisian sidewalk café by the atmosphere and flavors, which makes for an unforgettable dining experience.

Mediterranean Cuisine:
Savor Mediterranean cuisine at eateries that serve dishes from Greece, Spain, and other countries. Mediterranean cuisine is best characterized by a symphony of flavors created by fresh seafood, aromatic herbs, and olive oils. Savor outdoor dining that brings back memories of Mediterranean coastal villages.

Asian Noodle Bowls and Sushi:
Take in the rich diversity of Asian cuisine at Playa del Carmen's restaurants, which serve food from China, Japan, Thailand, and other countries. Taste the umami of well-prepared sushi, savor fragrant noodle bowls, and

appreciate the subtle harmony of flavors found in Far Eastern-inspired cuisine.

Steakhouses:
The bold tastes of a perfectly grilled steak are available at Playa del Carmen's steakhouses, which are a carnivorous delight. Enjoy perfectly cooked prime cuts paired with a variety of wines from around the world. The atmosphere evokes the sophistication of a vintage steakhouse, making for an unforgettable meal.

Vegetarian and Vegan Havens:
Playa del Carmen offers a wide selection of vegetarian and vegan eateries to suit a range of dietary requirements. These restaurants are inspired by world cuisines and serve delicious plant-based foods that highlight the diversity and inventiveness of vegetarian and vegan cooking.

The multicultural dining scene in Playa del Carmen is evidence of the town's allure. Every restaurant adds a different dimension to the culinary experience, whether you're enjoying the rustic flavors of an Italian trattoria or the delicate nuances of French cuisine. Allow your taste buds to lead you through the diverse range of flavors available, and let Playa del Carmen's international restaurants serve as a delightful culinary adventure.

Exploring Playa del Carmen's Streets' Culinary Tapestry

In addition to captivating visitors with its azure beaches, Playa del Carmen, a coastal gem on the Yucatán Peninsula, invites foodies to go on a street food exploration that reveals the real spirit of Mexican culinary culture. The town's street food scene is a lively fiesta of flavors, from vibrant markets to bustling street corners, inviting visitors to indulge in genuine dishes crafted by skilled hands and steeped in local traditions.

Tacos Al Pastor:
Tacos al pastor is a traditional Mexican dish that is a great way to start your street food exploration. A vertical spit expertly shaves spiced and marinated pork, encapsulating the essence of Middle Eastern influence on Mexican cuisine. A portable masterpiece is created by tucking these tasty morsels into soft corn tortillas and garnishing them with onions, cilantro, and a squeeze of lime.

Elote and Esquite:
The aromas of grilled corn on the cob and esquites (corn in a cup) will tantalize your senses. A symphony of flavors, including mayonnaise, cotija cheese, chili

powder, and lime juice, adorn these delicious street corn treats. Eaten on the cob or in a cup, elote and esquites represent the vibrant and flavorful aspect of Mexican street food.

Tamales:
Explore the cozy world of tamales, which are masa parcels that can be carried around and are filled with a variety of flavors, such as sweet fruits or savory meats. Tamale wrappers, made of corn husks or banana leaves, are a popular street snack that perfectly captures Mexico's culinary culture. For a true tamale experience, look for vendors with colorful displays and steaming pots.

Gorditas and Quesadillas:
Enjoy the ease of preparation and substantial nature of quesadillas and gorditas, which are stuffed with a variety of fillings such as cheese, meats, beans, and guacamole. These portable treats are a hit with both locals and tourists because they provide a delightful interplay of flavors and textures.

Marquesitas:
Marquesitas is a Yucatecan street snack that satisfies your sweet tooth by combining the crispiness of a crepe with the sweetness of Nutella, condensed milk, or any filling of your choice. Observe the process of spreading

the thin batter onto a griddle, adding your preferred toppings, and deftly folding it into a delightful cone of deliciousness.

Horchata and Frescas:
Quench your thirst with the vivid colors and crisp tastes of aguas frescas, a popular Mexican street food beverage made with fruit. These vibrant concoctions, which range from tamarind to hibiscus (Jamaica), are the ideal complement to your street food feast. Remember to sample horchata, a delightful and calming beverage made with sweet and creamy rice.

Churros & Chocolate:
Finish your exploration of street cuisine with the delightful satisfaction of chocolate and churros. Coated in cinnamon and sugar, these deep-fried dough treats are the ideal vehicle for dunks into a rich, velvety chocolate sauce. This delightful conclusion gives your street food exploration a hint of decadence.

The street food exploration of Playa del Carmen transports you to the core of Mexican culinary traditions through a colorful and flavorful journey. Every street food experience is an ode to Mexico's rich culinary history, from the savory dance of tacos al pastor to the sweet indulgence of churros. Thus, let the alluring scents lead you through the busy streets, and let Playa del

Carmen's cuisine become a treasured part of your culinary journey.

CHAPTER FIVE: SHOPPING

La Quinta Avenida: A Vibrant Cultural and Commercial Corridor in Playa del Carmen

La Quinta Avenida, or Fifth Avenue, weaves a colorful tapestry in the center of Playa del Carmen that captures the spirit of the town. This vibrant pedestrian street, which runs parallel to the Caribbean's crystal-clear shores, is a sensory extravaganza that provides a wide range of experiences, from retail therapy to cultural exploration, all against the backdrop of vibrant energy and charming coastal scenery.

Street Performances, Music, and Art:
Entering La Quinta Avenida transports you to a place where the past and present collide. The avenue is dotted with galleries that display the creations of regional and worldwide artists. Discover the colorful murals that adorn building facades and tell a story of Playa del Carmen's rich cultural diversity. The avenue's lively atmosphere is enhanced by street performers, musicians strumming guitars, and traditional dancers, who create an outdoor gallery of artistic expression.

A Shopping Heaven; From Market Stalls to Boutiques:
A shopping haven with a wide variety of boutiques, gift shops, and market stalls, La Quinta Avenida is a haven for bargain hunters. The avenue offers something for every taste and budget, whether you're looking for handcrafted Mexican crafts, fashionable beachwear, or unique trinkets to commemorate your journey. Explore the lively markets where craftspeople exhibit their work, offering a wide range of items from finely crafted silver jewelry to intricately woven textiles.

Culinary Treats; From Gourmet Dining to Street Food:
La Quinta Avenida becomes a gourmet haven when the sun goes down. The avenue offers something for every taste, from fine dining establishments with international cuisines to street food vendors selling delicious tacos and elotes. You can enjoy delicious food while taking in the vibrant atmosphere of the town at sidewalk cafes and rooftop restaurants, which offer a front-row seat to the bustling street scene.

Nightlife Hub; Rooftop Lounges, Clubs, and Bars:
La Quinta Avenida becomes the vibrant center of Playa del Carmen's nightlife as dusk approaches. Diverse nightlife is offered by hip bars with well-made cocktails, beach clubs with live music, and rooftop lounges with expansive views. The avenue fulfills all of your

nocturnal desires, whether you're looking for a dance-filled night in a lively club or a relaxed evening with live music.

Mayan Influences:
La Quinta Avenida honors the Mayan ancestry of the area. You will come across sculptures and art installations that demonstrate the influence of the ancient civilization at different points along the avenue. These nods to local culture blend in perfectly with the modern energy of the busy avenue, serving as a constant reminder of the town's strong ties to the Mayan heritage.

Access to the Beach and Coastal Walks:
Playa del Carmen's main thoroughfare, La Quinta Avenida, melds perfectly with the town's coastal charm. There are plenty of beach access points that make it easy to move from the bustling street scene to the calm Caribbean beaches. Enjoy the sound of the sea as you relax or take a stroll along the beach while observing the waves caress the sand.

More than just a street, La Quinta Avenida embodies the spirit of Playa del Carmen. The avenue is a dynamic entity that embodies this coastal haven, whether you're dancing the night away, enjoying culinary delights, soaking up its cultural treasures, or engaging in some retail therapy. So let La Quinta Avenida's vibrant energy lead the way as you explore, and let it be the vibrant thread that weaves your Playa del Carmen experience into an unforgettable and rich tapestry.

Playa del Carmen's Boutiques and Markets

Nestled along the Caribbean's turquoise shores, Playa del Carmen is not only a sun-drenched paradise but also a shopping enthusiast's dream come true for those looking for one-of-a-kind finds and locally made crafts. The town's markets and boutiques create a retail scene that artfully combines artistic flair with coastal charm to provide an out-of-the-ordinary shopping experience.

La Quinta Avenida:
La Quinta Avenida is the premier boutique destination in the center of Playa del Carmen. This lively pedestrian area is dotted with an amazing collection of boutiques, each of which offers a carefully chosen assortment of jewelry, clothing, and artwork. The boutiques along La Quinta Avenida feature a fusion of local and international designs, from stylish beachwear to handcrafted accessories, creating a fashion-forward atmosphere against the backdrop of lively street life.

Paseo del Carmen:

Paseo del Carmen, a waterfront shopping oasis next to La Quinta Avenida, elevates your retail experience with a dash of coastal elegance. Boutiques in this area offer a carefully chosen assortment of high-end clothing, beachwear, and handcrafted items. Take in the views of the Caribbean while strolling along the waterfront promenade and perusing these boutiques for an opulent and relaxed shopping experience.

Mamita's Village:
Mamita's Village is a hidden treasure waiting to be discovered by those who enjoy bohemian chic. This cluster of boutiques is tucked away from the main thoroughfares, giving it a relaxed and artistic atmosphere. Explore distinctive items, such as flowing sundresses and handcrafted jewelry, while strolling down Mamita's Village's quaint streets.

Quinta Alegria Shopping Center:
With a selection of boutique shops that appeal to a discerning clientele, Quinta Alegria Shopping Mall provides a contemporary shopping experience. This stylish mall brings together local and international brands, offering a welcome respite for those looking for a modern twist on sophistication amidst the beachy atmosphere of Playa del Carmen.

Artisan Markets:

Beyond the upscale shops, Playa del Carmen's artisan markets give your shopping expedition a more genuine feel. These markets feature a kaleidoscope of handcrafted treasures, like the lively and bustling Playa del Carmen Market. These markets provide a direct link to the artisans and their rich cultural legacy, showcasing everything from colorful ceramics to intricately woven textiles and traditional Mexican crafts.

Cozumel:
Cozumel, a short ferry ride away, broadens the shopping experience with its unique fusion of local markets and boutiques. The island's capital, San Miguel, is home to boutique stores with distinctive souvenirs, handcrafted jewelry, and island-chic clothing. Discover the artisanal spirit of Cozumel by perusing the local markets, where proud craftspeople display their creations.

Playa del Carmen is a retail haven with boutiques and markets that turn every walk into a treasure hunt. The town's shopping scene is a testament to its vibrant and diverse character, whether you're exploring bohemian finds in Mamita's Village, unearthing artisanal gems in local markets, or indulging in the chic offerings along La Quinta Avenida. Allow Playa del Carmen's boutiques and markets to create a unique and unforgettable experience for you while you explore these retail havens while enjoying the sea breeze.

Playa del Carmen Souvenirs and Unusual Finds

Traveling to Playa del Carmen offers the chance to bring a bit of Mexico's lively culture and coastal charm home with you, offering more than just a beachside getaway. The town offers a treasure trove of keepsakes that perfectly capture the spirit of your trip thanks to its eclectic selection of souvenirs and one-of-a-kind finds. Discover and treasure the ideal mementos of your seaside journey at Playa del Carmen, whether you're drawn to handcrafted goods, artistic creations, or souvenirs with a beach theme.

Traditional Mexican Handicrafts:
Playa del Carmen offers easy access to Mexico's renowned artisan culture, and local handicrafts make classic mementos. Look for colorful ceramics, handcrafted leather goods, and intricately woven textiles in markets and boutiques. While embroidered textiles highlight the artistry of Mexican craftsmanship, Talavera pottery, a distinctive style adorned with intricate patterns, makes for a striking and culturally significant keepsake.

Mayan Influenced Art:

Discover the artistic legacy of the Mayan civilization through one-of-a-kind artifacts that were influenced by historical patterns. Look for colorful paintings that portray Mayan scenes, handcrafted jewelry with symbols evoking this ancient culture, and intricately carved wooden masks. These works of art are not only exquisite decorations, but they also provide a link to the area's rich past.

Hammocks:
Add a traditional Mexican hammock to your home to add a bit of coastal relaxation. Hammocks, which are practical and evocative of the carefree lifestyle that is associated with Playa del Carmen, are handwoven with vivid colors and durable materials. They serve as a cozy reminder of carefree beach days and the calming sound of the trade winds from the Caribbean.

Lucia Libre Masks:
A Lucha Libre mask would make a unique and quirky memento. These intricate and colorful masks honor the colorful world of Mexican wrestling. A Lucha Libre mask adds a playful touch to your collection of mementos, whether you're a wrestling enthusiast or just looking for a distinctive and eye-catching memento.

Beach-Inspired Keepsakes:

Playa del Carmen's coastal charm is evident in its assortment of beach-themed mementos. Tangible recollections of the town's picturesque beaches include sand dollars, seashells, and coral fragments that have been fashioned into jewelry or decorative pieces. Seascapes and driftwood sculptures are just two examples of beach-themed artworks that perfectly capture the spirit of coastal living and add charm to your collection of mementos.

Local Artwork:
The galleries and artisan stores of Playa del Carmen are vibrant hubs of the artistic community. Think about purchasing original artwork created by regional artists, such as photographs that capture the distinct charm of the town or paintings and sculptures. These pieces of art support the thriving arts community that adds to Playa del Carmen's rich cultural tapestry in addition to being sentimental keepsakes.

Personalized Keepsakes:
Look into the option of customized items for a genuinely one-of-a-kind and personalized memento. Personalized engraving and embroidery services are provided by numerous local shops and artisans. A bespoke artwork, a piece of jewelry with your name on it, or an item painted specifically for you—a personalized souvenir guarantees

that your memories of Playa del Carmen will be etched into a unique memento.

Playa del Carmen's selection of mementos and unusual discoveries beckons you to transform your trip experiences into heirlooms. Every item you select, whether it be a personalized memento, a traditional craft, or artwork with Mayan influences, adds a new chapter to the tale of your voyage around the Caribbean. So, take your time perusing the markets, shops, and galleries, and allow Playa del Carmen's mementos to serve as enduring reminders of the idyllic beach town you experienced while visiting.

CHAPTER SIX: EXCURSIONS

Exploring Cozumel Island

Tucked away in the blue embrace of the Caribbean Sea, Cozumel Island entices visitors with a confluence of breathtaking scenery, an abundant marine ecosystem, and a wealth of cultural experiences. This tropical paradise, just a short ferry ride from Playa del Carmen, is a refuge for adventurers and those looking for some downtime. With its immaculate beaches and vibrant coral reefs, Cozumel has a wide range of activities to suit every preference.

Scuba Diving and Snorkeling Pleasures:
Underwater enthusiasts have an underwater playground in Cozumel's crystal-clear waters. The island is well known for offering top-notch scuba and snorkeling experiences. Discover the vibrant coral formations of the Columbia and Palancar reefs, where rays, schools of tropical fish, and occasionally even sea turtles gracefully move through the underwater scenery. Cozumel is a great place for beginners to dive because of its calm shallows, qualified instructors, and exciting dive sites.

Chankanaab National Park:

In the breathtaking coastal setting of Chankanaab National Park, culture and nature come together. Explore replicas of ancient Mayan structures, stroll through botanical gardens that highlight the region's diverse flora, and see playful dolphins in the park's dolphinarium. The park is a well-rounded destination for those looking for a mix of natural beauty and cultural immersion because it also offers fantastic snorkeling opportunities.

Punta Sur Eco Beach Park:
Punta Sur Eco Beach Park offers a pure and wild coastal experience. This ecological reserve supports a variety of ecosystems, including lagoons and mangroves. For sweeping views of the island and the Caribbean Sea, ascend to the top of Celarain Lighthouse. Discover the beaches of the park, where sea turtles lay their eggs, and take in the peace of this unspoiled beach retreat.

San Miguel:
The main town of Cozumel, San Miguel, has a relaxed charm that is accentuated by its lively colors, busy markets, and waterfront promenade. Look around the stores and boutiques that sell handmade jewelry, island-chic clothing, and souvenirs from the area. Savor the regional cuisine at restaurants by the sea, where traditional Mexican dishes and fresh seafood highlight the flavors of the area.

El Cedral:

El Cedral is a tiny village on Cozumel that is deeply ingrained in history. See the fusion of Spanish and Mayan influences at the El Cedral Mayan Ruins, one of the island's oldest archaeological sites. Take part in the vibrant El Cedral Festival celebration of Cozumel's cultural heritage through traditional music, dance, and religious ceremonies if your visit falls in late April.

Playa Mia Grand Beach Park:

A variety of family-friendly activities are available at Playa Mia Grand Beach Park for an enjoyable day out. Enjoy a swim in the pools, unwind on the immaculate beach, or participate in water sports. In addition, the park has a floating park, water slides, and mouthwatering food options. It's the ideal location for people looking for a lively, friendly environment with a blend of adventure and relaxation.

Bike or Moped Exploration:

By renting a bike or moped, you can explore Cozumel at your speed. Savor the island's natural beauty as you travel the coastal roads and discover undiscovered beaches. You can embrace the relaxed pace of island life with this mode of exploration, which comes with a gentle breeze and the sound of the sea as your companion.

Cozumel Island is a tropical haven where leisure and adventure coexist harmoniously. Cozumel invites you to design your island paradise, whether you're taking in the stunning beaches, diving into the vibrant underwater world, or just taking in the culture. Take a ferry ride from Playa del Carmen, allow the island's charm to reveal itself to you, and enjoy the special fusion of adventure and peace that characterizes Cozumel's coastal appeal.

Exploring Tulum Town

Tulum, a destination that seamlessly combines the allure of bohemian beach life with the mystery of ancient Mayan ruins, is perched majestically along the Riviera Maya. This seaside town welcomes visitors to enter a world where modernity and history coexist peacefully, with its immaculate beaches, turquoise waters, and well-preserved archaeological wonders.

Tulum Archaeological Site:
The archaeological site at Tulum, which bears witness to the sophisticated Maya civilization, is the city's crown jewel. The ruins of Tulum, which overlook the Caribbean Sea, offer a fascinating historical tour. Admire the magnificent murals at the Temple of the Frescoes and

the recognizable El Castillo, the main pyramid. With spectacular views of the coast, the archaeological site provides a unique chance to investigate the ruins of a prosperous Mayan city.

Beautiful Beaches:
The beaches of Tulum are picture-perfect, with soft white sand meeting soft Caribbean waves. Chic, eco-friendly resorts, boutique hotels, and rustic cabanas dot the beachfront. Tulum's beaches radiate a carefree, bohemian vibe that encourages rest and renewal, whether you're practicing yoga on the sand or relaxing in a hammock slung between palm trees.

Cenotes:
Go inland to explore Tulum's cenotes, which are natural wonders. The cool freshwater in these sinkholes is a welcome diversion from the seaside heat. Enjoy a swim or a snorkel in these hallowed pools that are encircled by stalactites, stalagmites, and lush vegetation. Popular options for people looking for a peaceful and dreamlike cenote experience are Gran Cenote and Dos Ojos.

Biosphere Reserve of San Ka'an:
A visit to the Sian Ka'an Biosphere Reserve is essential for anyone who loves the outdoors. This UNESCO World Heritage Site is home to a variety of ecosystems, such as forests, wetlands, and barrier reefs. Experience a

boat tour of the reserve to see the diverse array of plants and animals. Observing rare species will be a thrill for birdwatchers, and the lagoons and mangroves enhance the ecological appeal of the reserve.

Tulum Pueblo:
The town center, Tulum Pueblo, provides a taste of local life beyond the beaches and ruins. Discover the lively streets filled with artisanal markets, boutique stores, and murals painted in vibrant colors. Savor Mexican cuisine at neighborhood restaurants where the aromas of traditional cooking fill the air. Away from the tranquility of the coast, Tulum Pueblo offers a window into the everyday charm of the community.

Wellness and Yoga Retreats:
The world has come to recognize Tulum as a center for holistic living and wellness. Holistic spas, yoga studios, and wellness retreats are scattered throughout the town. Take a yoga class on the beach, treat yourself to a holistic spa treatment, or go on a health retreat that feeds your body and soul. The tranquil surroundings of Tulum provide the ideal setting for anyone looking for a complete getaway.

Street Art Galleries and Murals:
The vibrant murals and street art that cover Tulum's streets add to the town's bohemian charm. The walls are

adorned by the works of both local and foreign artists, transforming the space into an outdoor gallery that enhances Tulum's cultural offerings. Take a stroll through the streets to uncover the town's creative spirit's expressive and eclectic side.

Explore the nexus of natural beauty, ancient history, and contemporary bohemian living in Tulum. Tulum is a place that exudes a timeless and transforming energy, whether you're exploring the ruins with views of the Caribbean, relaxing on the immaculate beaches, or taking in the town's holistic and artistic offerings. So, as you journey along the sun-kissed shores of the Riviera Maya, let the whispers of the ancient Maya guide you and let Tulum weave its entrancing tapestry of history, nature, and culture.

Playa del Carmen Cenote Exploration

Located on the sunny Yucatán Peninsula, Playa del Carmen is more than just a beach haven; it serves as a doorway to the fascinating cenotes, a hidden realm below the surface. For those looking for an escape from the coastal heat and an exploration of nature's underground wonders, these naturally occurring sinkholes, with their glistening waters and historic geological formations, present a singular and captivating experience.

Geological Wonders of Nature:
Cenotes, which are created when limestone bedrock collapses, reveal an amazing network of clear groundwater-filled caves and caverns beneath the surface. There is a vast network of these geological marvels throughout the Yucatán Peninsula, which includes the Playa del Carmen region. Each has its unique charm and personality. The stories of cenotes are as fascinating as they are varied, featuring everything from sunlight-drenched outdoor cenotes to secret caverns shrouded in mystery.

Cenote Azul:
Discoverers are invited to explore Cenote Azul, which is only a short drive from Playa del Carmen and boasts pure waters encircled by lush vegetation. The cenote's name, "azul," which translates to "blue" in Spanish, aptly describes the vibrant colors of its waters. In this breathtaking natural setting, you can swim or snorkel and discover fascinating underwater rock formations as well as the occasional fish swimming through the transparent depths.

Cenote Cristalino:

Cenote Cristalino provides a peaceful haven for those seeking peace. Encircled by lush tropical vegetation, this hidden gem beckons guests to relax in its tranquil atmosphere. Cenote Cristalino, whether surface-diving or plunging into its cool depths, is a monument to the elegance and simplicity found in nature's embrace.

Cenote Chaak Tun:
For an adventure off the beaten path, head to Cenote Chaak Tun to avoid the crowds. With its stalactite and stalagmite decorations, this network of underground caverns carries visitors to a mystical realm. You can explore the complex formations and discover the geological past that shaped these fascinating underground marvels by taking guided tours.

Jardin del Eden Cenote:
As its name suggests, Jardin del Eden Cenote is a secret garden just waiting to be discovered. Surrounded by lush vegetation, the open-air cenote creates a natural oasis where guests can enjoy the dappled sunlight that filters through the leaves. Dive into the refreshing waters and take in the captivating cenote's composition of light and shadow.

Cenote Dos Ojos:
With its vast cave system, Cenote Dos Ojos, just a short drive from Playa del Carmen, entices scuba divers. The

name, which translates to "Two Eyes" in Spanish, alludes to the two interconnected sinkholes that open up to a maze-like underwater environment. Dos Ojos provides an immersive dive into the mysteries of the cenote realm, perfect for both novice and expert snorkelers.

Cenote Discovery Advice:
To ensure a smooth experience when exploring cenotes in Playa del Carmen, take into account the following advice:
- Guided Tours: Choose a guided tour to learn about each cenote's safety procedures, cultural significance, and geological past.
- Swimwear and Snorkel Gear: To completely immerse yourself in the underwater wonders, pack comfortable swimwear and snorkel gear.
- Biodegradable Sunscreen: To save the fragile ecosystem surrounding the cenotes, use a biodegradable sunscreen.
- Respect Nature: Be a responsible traveler by not interfering with the wildlife and natural formations in and around the cenotes.

Discovering Playa del Carmen's cenotes is a journey into the underground wonders of nature. Every cenote reveals a different aspect of this hidden world, whether you decide to dive into Cenote Dos Ojos or float in the serene waters of Cenote Cristalino. To fully experience the Yucatán Peninsula, give in to the allure of the underground oasis, let the cenotes serve as your entryway to exploration, and let Playa del Carmen's geological wonders become a memorable part of your journey.

A Week-End Vacation in Playa del Carmen: An Exciting 7-Day Schedule

Playa del Carmen invites visitors to partake in a varied and enriching experience with its sun-kissed beaches, lively culture, and breathtaking natural features. This well-planned 7-day itinerary makes sure that every day in this coastal paradise is full of special experiences by providing the ideal balance of leisure, adventure, and cultural exploration.

Day 1: Welcome and Arrival at the Beachfront:

- Morning: Get to Playa del Carmen and make yourself at home.
- Afternoon: Visit Playa Mamitas, a famous beach in the town. Enjoy beachside refreshments, swim in the blue waters, and unwind on the fine sand.
- Evening: Take a stroll down Quinta Avenida, also known as Fifth Avenue, where lively eateries, boutiques,

and stores come to life. Savor your first taste of authentic Mexican food from the area.

Day 2: Tulum's Mayan Marvels

- Morning: Explore the Tulum Archaeological Site, where you can gaze in awe at the prehistoric Mayan ruins set against the Caribbean Sea.
- Afternoon: Take in Tulum's bohemian charm while lounging on the beach. Shop locally and enjoy seafood specialties at restaurants by the beach.
- Evening: Take in Tulum's nightlife, with bars and beach clubs providing a blend of live music and a beachside atmosphere.

Day 3: Nature Retreat and Cenote Exploration:

- Morning: Explore the cenotes. For a revitalizing swim in the glistening natural pools, pick Cenote Azul or Cenote Cristalino.
- Afternoon: Rejuvenate your body and mind with a wellness retreat or spa day.
- Evening: Savor fresh seafood at a restaurant by the sea while watching the sunset over the Caribbean.

Day 4: Island Adventure on Cozumel:

- Morning: Travel to Cozumel Island by ferry. Discover the main town, San Miguel, and go to the markets to buy handcrafted goods.
- Afternoon: Take a snorkeling or diving excursion along Cozumel's colorful reefs to explore the underwater wonders.
- Evening: Savor a meal by the sea while taking in the relaxed ambiance of the island.

Day 5: Playa del Carmen Cultural Day:

- Morning: Discover Playa del Carmen's murals and local art galleries. For a taste of Mexican artistry, head to the Frida Kahlo Museum.
- Afternoon: Explore the town's rich cultural legacy by going to the Maya Culture Museum or the 3D Museum of Wonders.
- Evening: For a fully immersive cultural experience, catch a live performance or traditional dance show.

Day 6: Sian Ka'an Nature Expedition:

- Morning: A guided tour to Sian Ka'an Biosphere Reserve will begin in the morning. Take a boat tour through the mangroves, observe wildlife, and explore the various ecosystems.
- Afternoon: Have lunch at a neighborhood restaurant inside the reserve or have a beach picnic.

- Evening: Head back to Playa del Carmen and relax with a stroll along the beach as the sun sets.

Day 7: Unwinding and Leaving:
Autumn: Savor a leisurely breakfast at a cafe by the sea.
- Afternoon: Savor the sun, sea, and sand as you spend your final day at the beach. Go on a catamaran cruise or engage in some water sports.
- Evening: Have a farewell dinner and reflect on the week's highlights as you wrap up your adventures in Playa del Carmen.

This 7-day itinerary combines natural wonders, historical sites, cultural exploration, and leisure to provide a well-rounded experience of Playa del Carmen. Discovering historic sites, exploring underground caves, and enjoying regional cuisine are just a few of the adventures that await you every day in this idyllic coastal destination. Adapt the schedule to your tastes, and allow Playa del Carmen to enchant you throughout your entire week-long visit.

CHAPTER SEVEN: PRACTICAL TIPS

Crucial Rules for a Safe Visit in Playa del Carmen

Travelers looking for adventures in the sun are drawn to Playa del Carmen because of its gorgeous beaches and lively culture. Safety must come first to guarantee a safe and enjoyable stay. Here are some important safety precautions you should take while visiting this coastal paradise.

1. Health Safety Measures:

Insurance for Travel: Get comprehensive travel insurance that covers unanticipated events and medical emergencies before you depart.

Wellness Exam: Keep yourself updated about any travel warnings issued by relevant authorities, as well as the local health guidelines.

Medical Facilities: Keep a basic first aid kit on hand in case of minor medical emergencies, and be aware of the locations of adjacent pharmacies and medical facilities.

2. Safety at the Beach:

Warning About Swimming: Keep an eye out for warning flags and be aware of ocean currents. Swim in areas designated for lifeguards, and follow their instructions.

Sun Protection: Use sunglasses, hats, and sunscreen to shield your skin from the sun. Particularly during the hours of greatest sunlight, stay hydrated.

3. Water and Cenote Activities:

Expert Counseling: When participating in water sports such as snorkeling or cenote exploration, choose reliable tour companies that have trained guides and security measures in place.

Life Jackets: Make sure that life jackets are available and used appropriately, particularly for activities where they are suggested or necessary.

4. Security of Transportation:

Authorized Services: Select reliable and licensed transportation providers. Use authorized transportation hubs and verify the credentials of taxi drivers.

Backrest Belts: In cars, buckle up at all times. Learn the traffic laws in the area if you're renting a car.

5. Personal Security and Valuables:

Secure Belongings: Keep valuables hidden and keep your belongings safe. Passports, cash, and other important documents should be kept in hotel safes.

Safety at Night: When you go exploring at night, use caution. Remain in well-lit areas and make use of reliable transit sources.

6. Regional Laws and Customs:

Respect Local Customs: To guarantee a courteous and pleasurable experience, familiarize yourself with local customs and etiquette.

Legal Awareness: Recognize and abide by all applicable local laws and ordinances, including those about recreational activities and alcohol consumption.

7. Being Ready for Emergencies:

Contacts for Emergencies: Keep a phone list of local emergency numbers handy, along with the number of the closest embassy or consulate.

Communication Plan: Make plans with your traveling companions for communication. Throughout your visit, stay in touch by sharing your itinerary.

The secret to a wonderful and worry-free vacation in Playa del Carmen is to put safety first. You can enjoy every second of your journey in this alluring coastal destination by being informed, making responsible decisions, and adhering to local regulations. Let safety be your constant companion during your Playa del Carmen adventure, whether you're exploring cenotes, relaxing on the beach, or taking in the local way of life.

Playa del Carmen Local Etiquette

Adopting local etiquette before setting out on your Playa del Carmen adventure is not only polite but also essential to gaining access to genuine experiences and developing deep relationships with the kind residents. This guide will help you ensure that your interactions in this coastal haven are as rich in culture and enriching as the destination itself by explaining the subtleties of social grace.

1. Salutations and Etiquette:

Hey, how are you? It is customary to strike up a conversation with an amiable "Hola". A friendly smile goes a long way toward communicating friendliness, and handshakes are customary.

Politeness Is Important: Courtesies are highly esteemed. It is customary to use "por favor" (please) and "gracias" (thank you) in interactions, whether they take place in restaurants, retail establishments, or casual encounters.

2. Touch and Personal Space:

Spatial Respect: In general, Mexicans value having a comfortable conversational distance. Although loving gestures are typical between friends and family, it's advisable to respect personal space when interacting with strangers.

A heartfelt greeting: Cheek kisses are a common social gesture among friends and family. If you follow the locals' example, a quick cheek-to-cheek touch will do.

3. Table manners:

Laidback Ambience: Playa del Carmen is known for its laid-back dining scene. Savor the flavors of your meals and converse with others in a relaxed and conversational manner.

Custom of Tipping: In restaurants, tipping is customary and usually consists of 10% to 15% of the total bill. Be advised that certain places might charge a service fee.

4. Attire Requirement:

Beach Casual: Playa del Carmen has a relaxed atmosphere, particularly in the vicinity of the beach. It is appropriate to dress casually with sandals, sundresses, and shorts. A little more polished look, though, might be valued in more formal settings.

In-Town Coverage: If you venture off the beach, think about wearing more clothing. While bathers are appropriate at the beach, it is courteous to change into cover-ups or appropriate clothing when exploring the town.

5. Market Bargaining:

Respectful Negotiation: In local markets, haggling is typical. Be kind and respectful when dealing with it.

Remember that the final cost is frequently the result of compromises.

6. Respect for Language:

Try These Spanish Words: Even though English is widely spoken by residents of Playa del Carmen, trying out a few simple Spanish words and phrases like "por favor" and "gracias" is appreciated.

Level Adjustment: When conversing in public areas, keeping the volume down demonstrates consideration for other people.

7. Holidays and Festivities:

Take Part Enthusiastically: If your trip coincides with a holiday or celebration in the area, get fully involved. When taking pictures during religious ceremonies, please ask permission and show respect for the customs and traditions of the area.

8. Concern for the Environment:

Eco-Friendly Mentality: Playa del Carmen values protecting the environment. Get involved in environmentally friendly projects and ethically dispose of waste.

Accepting the customs of the locals in Playa del Carmen will improve your vacation experience and make you feel like a valued member of the colorful fabric of Mexican culture. Let civility and respect dictate your interactions, whether you're dining by the sea, strolling along Quinta Avenida, or interacting with locals in markets. These experiences will leave you with enduring memories of a trip where cultural exchange is just as enriching as the destination itself.

Playa del Carmen's Medical Facilities and Health Precautions

While enjoying Playa del Carmen's sun-kissed shores, keeping your health and well-being in mind should be your first concern. This guide gives you information on health precautions, accessible medical facilities, and crucial details so you can plan your stay with confidence.

1. Health Safety Measures:

Insurance for Travel: Get comprehensive travel insurance before you leave on your trip, covering hospitalization and evacuation in the event of a medical emergency.

Vaccinations: For advice on recommended vaccinations for travel to Mexico, consult your healthcare provider. Hepatitis A and B, typhoid, and routine vaccinations are among the common vaccines.

Water and Food Safety: Use caution when consuming street food, and limit your intake to well-cooked or peeled fruits and vegetables. Remain with purified or bottled water and steer clear of ice in beverages from unknown sources.

2. Healthcare Facilities:

Medical Facilities: Internationally compliant modern medical facilities can be found in Playa del Carmen. Costumed and Hospiten Riviera Maya are two renowned hospitals.

Pharmacies: Known as "farmacias," pharmacies are widely distributed and offer a variety of prescription and over-the-counter drugs. Common chains are Farmacias del Ahorro and Farmacias Similares.

3. Help for Emergencies:

Calls for emergencies: To get medical help in an emergency, dial 911. Some operators speak English, and they can point you in the direction of the right services.

Medical Transport Services: Emergency medical transportation is readily provided by private companies such as Hospiten and local Red Cross facilities, as well as ambulance services.

4. Physicians who Speak English:

Health Care Practitioners: In Playa del Carmen, a large number of medical professionals speak English fluently. This facilitates communication for travelers who need medical care.

Hotel Support: Hotels can help guests connect with English-speaking doctors if necessary, as they frequently maintain relationships with local medical professionals.

5. Drugstores and Prescription Items:

Medications on Prescription: Make sure you pack enough prescription medication for your trip if you need it. Get acquainted with the generic names as well because brand names can vary.

Hours of Pharmacy: Pharmacies usually have extended business hours, which include weekends and evenings. Renowned choices include Farmacia Paris and Farmacia del Carmen.

6. Health Kit for Travelers:

First Aid Package: Stow basic first aid supplies in a kit that includes bandages, antiseptic wipes, painkillers, and any prescription drugs you may have.

Sun Shielding: It's essential to wear sunglasses, hats, and sunscreen to protect yourself from the intense Mexican sun.

7. Retreats for Health and Wellbeing:

Health Facilities: Numerous holistic health services and wellness retreats can be found in Playa del Carmen. For rejuvenation, think about treating yourself to spa services, yoga classes, or wellness initiatives.

Putting your health first in Playa del Carmen means being aware of local medical resources, taking preventative steps, and being ready for anything that might come up. You can travel the coast with confidence, knowing that this energetic Mexican destination will support your well-being, if you are familiar with these health guidelines.

CHAPTER EIGHT: TRANSPORTATION

Transportation Within Playa del Carmen

The convenience of transportation becomes a crucial aspect of your vacation experience as soon as you arrive in Playa del Carmen, a bustling coastal paradise. This guide offers insights into the various transportation options available, so every part of this sun-drenched destination is accessible, from sandy beaches to bustling markets.

Public Transportation:
- Collectivos: Shared vans that run on set routes are known as "colectivos," and they're a well-liked and reasonably priced form of transportation. For short trips within Playa del Carmen or neighboring towns, they're perfect.

- Local Buses: Playa del Carmen offers affordable transportation throughout the town through its local bus system. For buses that go into the town center, look for those with the "Centro" label.

Chauffeur Services:
Official Taxis: Make use of authorized taxi services at predetermined prices. Taxis are a practical choice for short distances and are widely accessible throughout Playa del Carmen.

Negotiating Fares: Although official taxis have set prices, it's a good idea to check the fare with the driver before setting out on your trip, particularly if you're going somewhere outside of the town center.

Car Rental:
Car Rental Agencies: Playa del Carmen is home to several car rental companies for those wishing to independently explore the surrounding areas. Make sure you are knowledgeable about the local traffic laws and that you have the required paperwork.

Parking: If you are renting a car, make sure to inquire about parking options from your lodging; some hotels offer parking.

Cycling:
Eco-Friendly Exploration: Rent a bicycle to fully embrace Playa del Carmen's environmentally conscious vibe. Bicycles are available for rent from several local businesses, making them an eco-friendly and leisurely mode of transportation.

Bike Paths: There are specific bike paths in some places, particularly those close to the beach. When riding a bicycle on the road, use caution and follow all traffic laws.

On Foot Exploration:
Beachside Walks: The main attractions in Playa del Carmen are frequently reachable on foot, particularly along the beach. Take strolls and leisurely explorations of the shoreline.

Comfortable Attire: Wear appropriate footwear for walking on various terrains and dress comfortably in light of the tropical climate.

Cozumel Ferry:
Island Adventure: The ferry service from Playa del Carmen offers a convenient and scenic journey if you're planning a trip to Cozumel. Ferries provide breathtaking views of the Caribbean Sea and run on a regular schedule.

Ferry Terminals: In Playa del Carmen, there are two ferry terminals: one at Calle 1 and the beach, and the other close to the Cozumel Maritime Terminal.

Ride-sharing Companies:

App-Based Rides: In Playa del Carmen, ridesharing services such as Uber function as a substitute for conventional taxis. Enjoy the convenience of cashless transactions by downloading the app.

Playa del Carmen transportation is a smooth and delightful aspect of the experience. There are plenty of ways to get around Playa del Carmen, whether you want to take a stroll down Quinta Avenida, experience the local charm of colectivos, or go on a coastal bike ride. Allow the adventure to begin as you explore this sun-kissed location and learn about its treasures while enjoying the independence and adaptability that come with using a variety of modes of transportation.

Playa del Carmen Car Rentals and Transportation Services

Having the flexibility to move at your speed makes exploring Playa del Carmen's sun-drenched landscapes and cultural attractions even more enthralling. This guide provides a road map for freedom and convenience in this coastal paradise by revealing the options for vehicle rentals and transportation services.

Auto Rental Companies:

Freedom to Explore: Renting a car in Playa del Carmen gives visitors the freedom to independently discover the Yucatán Peninsula and all of its many attractions. Hertz, Avis, and Mex Rent a Car are just a few of the many local and international car rental companies that operate in the area.

Booking Options: To guarantee your chosen vehicle type and a smooth pickup procedure when you arrive, it is advised that you reserve a car online in advance.

Playa del Carmen Driving:

Road Conditions: Playa del Carmen's road system is kept up nicely, with highways linking it to important destinations like Tulum, Cancún, and cenotes. Become familiar with local traffic laws and road signs.

Gas Stations: Gas stations are widely distributed and usually accept cash as payment. Before you go on longer trips, make sure your tank is full.

Parking Structures:

Hotel Parking: A lot of Playa del Carmen's hotels provide parking for visitors. Verify the availability of parking and any related costs with your lodging.

Street Parking: There are several locations where you can park on the street. To avoid fines, abide by parking regulations and park in designated spots.

Local Buses and Colectivos:

Cheap Transportation Options: Local buses and colectivos (shared vans) are affordable options for short trips within Playa del Carmen or neighboring towns.

Fixed Routes: Colectivos are a convenient option for traveling around town because they adhere to set routes. Their route signs and frequent stops along major roads identify them.

Chauffeur Services:

Convenience and Comfort: Within Playa del Carmen, taxis offer comfortable point-to-point transportation. They are easily found at hotels, taxi stands, and well-known tourist locations.

Official Taxi Rates: Based on zones, official taxis have set rates. Before you leave, especially for destinations outside the town center, confirm the fare with the driver.

In Playa del Carmen, car rentals and transportation services provide a range of options to suit different tastes and modes of transportation. Whether you like your travels to be as magical as the destination itself, or if you prefer the independence of a rental car, the affordability of colectivos, or the convenience of taxis, this coastal paradise has plenty of transportation options to suit your needs. So grab your seat and let the open roads of Playa del Carmen guide you to fascinating discoveries and life-changing experiences as you set out on a road trip adventure.

CHAPTER NINE: CELEBRATIONS

Playa del Carmen's Annual Celebrations

Beyond its immaculate beaches and historical sites, Playa del Carmen offers a plethora of cultural experiences. The town comes alive with a calendar of yearly events that highlight the vibrant dance, upbeat music, and rich traditions that characterize Mexican culture. This guide invites you to partake in the joyous celebration as it opens the pages of Playa del Carmen's festive journal.

Dia de los Muertos, or Day of the Dead
Respect for Culture: Day of the Dead is observed from October 31 to November 2 and is a somber yet joyous occasion that pays tribute to loved ones who have passed away. Take in colorful processions, elaborately decorated altars, and traditional fare that capture the essence of this emotional celebration.
Participation in the Community: With vibrant parades along Quinta Avenida, Playa del Carmen captures the spirit of Día de los Muertos. Both locals and tourists dress in traditional costumes and honor the deceased.

Rosario

Happy Holidays: Carnaval, which takes place in the days preceding Lent, turns the streets into a colorful, musical, and dancing carnival. Take part in the vibrant parades that have intricate floats, dancers, and upbeat music that create a thrilling atmosphere.

Dress to Impress: The colorful spectacle is enhanced by the colorful costumes, masks, and face paint worn by both locals and visitors. The celebrations enticingly invite everyone to partake in the joyful chaos that encapsulates the carefree spirit of Playa del Carmen.

The Day of Independence (Día de la Independencia)

Patriotic Magnificence: Independence Day, observed on September 16th, honors Mexico's proclamation of independence. Take in the magnificent Grito de Independencia ceremony, which includes patriotic music, speeches, and the customary "Viva México!" yell.

City Parties: Take part in the vibrant street celebrations, where the town is decked out in the Mexican flag's colors of green, white, and red. Savor regional cuisine, live music, and the friendship of people uniting to celebrate their country's past.

Jazz Festival at Riviera Maya

Harmonic Concord: The Riviera Maya Jazz Festival, which takes place every November, is a must-see event for fans of music. Renowned jazz musicians perform on the beachside stages, evoking a mesmerizing ambiance with their poignant tunes.

Seaside melodies: Imagine yourself beneath a starry sky while the soft sound of the waves crashes against the rhythmic sounds of jazz. Playa del Carmen is transformed into a music lover's paradise during the festival.

The Month of Mexican Independence

Celebration Over Several Months: September is a month-long celebration of Mexican Independence, not just one day. Savor unique occasions, musical performances, and cultural events that highlight the pride and solidarity of the Mexican people throughout September.

Concerts and Fireworks: The month comes to a close with grand firework displays, live concerts, and a joyful vibe that fills the streets and invites everyone to join in the fun.

Film Festival at Riviera Maya

Cinematic Splendor: During the summer, movie buffs can attend the Riviera Maya Film Festival. With the backdrop of the Caribbean, this event offers a wide range of domestic and international film selections, fostering a rich cultural experience.

Auctions Outside: Take advantage of outdoor movie screenings at several venues, such as the beach, for a distinctive cinematic experience under the stars.

The town of Playa del Carmen's lively culture and lively spirit are demonstrated by its yearly celebrations. Every celebration adds a layer of magic to your trip along the coast, whether you find yourself lost in the vibrant energy of Carnaval, paying respects on Día de los Muertos, or lost in the melodic notes of the Jazz Festival. Take part in the festivities with the locals, respect cultural differences, and allow Playa del Carmen's festive beats to serve as a relaxing background track for your travel experiences.

Playa del Carmen's Schedule of Local Events

The vibrant events calendar of Playa del Carmen elevates your vacation experience above and beyond the sun-kissed beaches and historical attractions. A plethora of artistic, musical, and cultural events take place all year long, captivating both locals and visitors and fostering a sense of celebration and solidarity. With the help of this thorough guide, you can explore the wide variety of events that Playa del Carmen has to offer and make sure you don't miss a thing while on your beach vacation.

Carnaval in Playa del Carmen
Time: February
Summary: Playa del Carmen's streets come alive with color, music, and dancing during Carnaval. The town is filled with festive chaos created by elaborate parades, masked revelers, and colorful costumes.

Film Festival at Riviera Maya
Time: May
Summary: Cinema fans celebrate the Riviera Maya Film Festival. The town is transformed into a cinematic paradise with a carefully chosen selection of national and international films shown in theaters and outdoor venues.

Travesía Sagrada Maya
Time: May
Summary: Join us as we retrace the ancient Mayas' maritime journey from Playa del Carmen to Cozumel, experiencing history brought to life. With all of its ceremonies and rituals, this cultural reenactment provides a deep window into the history of the area.

Jazz Festival at Riviera Maya
Time: November

Summary: The Riviera Maya Jazz Festival features soulful jazz notes accompanied by a gentle sea breeze. Famous performers perform under the stars on the beach, creating a unique musical experience.

Día de los Muertos (Day of the Dead)
Time: October 31–November 2
Summary: Playa del Carmen honors the memory of departed loved ones with colorful processions, elaborate altars, and regional cuisine. For the celebration of Día de los Muertos, Quinta Avenida turns into a vibrant canvas for both locals and tourists.

Celebraciones on Independence Day (Día de la Independencia)
Time: September 16th
Summary: Playa del Carmen is filled with patriotic energy as they celebrate Mexican Independence Day in September. This vibrant celebration is typified by the Grito de Independencia ceremony, street parties, and vibrant decorations.

Food & Wine Festival at Riviera Maya:
Time: April
Summary: At the Riviera Maya Food & Wine Festival, gourmets from around the world gather to demonstrate their culinary skills. There will be plenty of food

tastings, wine pairings, and culinary treats at this delicious event.

Seaside Rotary Club of Playa del Carmen Wine and Food Festival
Time: March
Summary: The Playa del Carmen Seaside Rotary Club Wine and Food Festival is a culinary extravaganza. In a gorgeous coastal setting, savor fine dining, fine wines, and live entertainment.

Underground Film Festival at Riviera Maya
Month: December
Summary: At the Riviera Maya Underground Film Festival, embrace the avant-garde. Independent and experimental films are screened at this event, giving up-and-coming filmmakers a chance to get their start.

Christmas Boat Parade in Playa del Carmen
Month: December
Summary: Take part in the Playa del Carmen Christmas Boat Parade to celebrate the holidays. Decorated boats ply the azure seas, lighting up the night with festivity and bringing happiness to the shoreline.

Mes de la Patria, or Mexican Independence Month
Time: September

Summary: September becomes a month-long celebration of Mexican heritage that lasts past Independence Day. Events, patriotic displays, and concerts bring residents and guests together in jubilant remembrance.

The vibrant events calendar of Playa del Carmen is a testament to the town's vibrancy and diversity of culture. Every event adds a unique color to your Playa del Carmen experience, whether you're dancing through the streets during Carnival, indulging in gourmet treats at a wine festival, or taking in the spiritual atmosphere of Día de los Muertos. Thus, plan your visit to coincide with the upbeat beats of these regional celebrations, and allow the town's colorful schedule to add memorable experiences and cultural significance to your seaside vacation.

CONCLUSION

Playa del Carmen is a coastal gem that shines in the center of the Yucatán Peninsula. Its allure goes well beyond the sun-drenched beaches and Mayan wonders that adorn its surroundings. A destination that beckons with a symphony of experiences, from the serene embrace of turquoise waters to the lively rhythm of Quinta Avenida. Not only is Playa del Carmen's environment breathtaking, but it also provides an immersive experience that transports visitors through Mexican history, culture, and liveliness.

Every step you take on the cobblestone streets feels like a dance with the past, a story etched in the ruins of Tulum and the sacred Mayan customs that reverberate throughout the area. It's a location where tradition and modernity coexist harmoniously to create a one-of-a-kind mosaic where celebrations from centuries past blend with those from the present.

Playa del Carmen's streets thump with the colorful energy of regional festivals and global events, while its beaches, with their fine sands and glistening waters, beckon you to bask in the embrace of the Caribbean. Every moment of your trip to Playa del Carmen contributes to the rich tapestry of your experience, whether you're lost in the rhythms of Carnaval, indulging in gourmet treats at a wine festival, or following the path of the revered Mayan pilgrimage.

This location is more than just a gorgeous setting; it's a blank canvas with a narrative written on every stroke. It's the vibrant local markets, the eerie allure of cenotes, and Quinta Avenida's rainbow of colors. It's the joyful shouts of "Viva México!" on Independence Day, the mellow sounds of jazz floating on the water, and the deeply emotional celebrations of Día de los Muertos every year.

More than just a place to visit, Playa del Carmen is an invitation to fully immerse yourself in a culture that is as vibrant, fragrant, and ingrained in Mexican culture as the petals of a bougainvillea in full bloom. Playa del Carmen reveals itself as a place that goes beyond the typical, leaving visitors with more than just memories—they leave with an enduring connection to the heart and soul of this coastal haven—from the bustling street scenes to the peaceful moments by the sea. Playa del Carmen whispers its story in every wave that laps the shore and in every beat that reverberates through the town. It's a story that beckons you to become more than just a spectator, but an active participant in the engrossing story of a place that is genuinely unique in every way.

Made in the USA
Las Vegas, NV
17 January 2024

84515957R00057